Put Beginning Readers on the Right Track with
ALL ABOARD READING™

The All Aboard Reading series is especially designed for beginning readers. Written by noted authors and illustrated in full color, these are books that children really want to read—books to excite their imagination, expand their interests, make them laugh, and support their feelings. With fiction and nonfiction stories that are high interest and curriculum-related, All Aboard Reading books offer something for every young reader. And with four different reading levels, the All Aboard Reading series lets you choose which books are most appropriate for your children and their growing abilities.

Picture Readers
Picture Readers have super-simple texts, with many nouns appearing as rebus pictures. At the end of each book are 24 flash cards—on one side is a rebus picture; on the other side is the written-out word.

Station Stop 1
Station Stop 1 books are best for children who have just begun to read. Simple words and big type make these early reading experiences more comfortable. Picture clues help children to figure out the words on the page. Lots of repetition throughout the text helps children to predict the next word or phrase—an essential step in developing word recognition.

Station Stop 2
Station Stop 2 books are written specifically for children who are reading with help. Short sentences make it easier for early readers to understand what they are reading. Simple plots and simple dialogue help children with reading comprehension.

Station Stop 3
Station Stop 3 books are perfect for children who are reading alone. With longer text and harder words, these books appeal to children who have mastered basic reading skills. More complex stories captivate children who are ready for more challenging books.

In addition to All Aboard Reading books, look for All Aboard Math Readers™ (fiction stories that teach math concepts children are learning in school) and All Aboard Science Readers™ (nonfiction books that explore the most fascinating science topics in age-appropriate language).

All Aboard for happy reading!

Library of Congress Cataloging-in-Publication Data is available.

ISBN 0-448-43342-7 (pbk)   A B C D E F G H I J

ISBN 0-448-43343-5 (GB)   A B C D E F G H I J

ALL ABOARD READING™

A HORSE NAMED Seabiscuit

By Mark and Cathy Dubowski
Illustrated by Mark Rowe
Includes photographs

Grosset & Dunlap • New York

Something was wrong with Seabiscuit.
He was the son of a great racehorse. His
grandfather was a famous racehorse. He
should have been a champion, too.

But Seabiscuit was a big disappointment.
In two years, in over 35 races, he had
never won. Not once.

Seabiscuit looked funny. He was small. His legs were short and his forelegs were crooked. He had a ragged little tail.

He ran funny, too. One writer said he ran like a duck. Others said he looked like an eggbeater when he galloped. Often he kicked his back legs with his front hooves.

And Seabiscuit misbehaved. His owner wanted to sell him. But nobody wanted a troublesome horse who never won.

Then one day, a quiet man came to the track to look at the horses. His name was Tom Smith. He was a horse trainer. Smith leaned on the fence and watched.

Jockeys were leading some horses to the starting post. Just then, one funny-looking, mud-colored horse looked Smith right in the eye. He liked the horse's spirit.

"I'll see you again," he told the horse.

And he did! Tom Smith convinced his boss, who owned racehorses, to buy Seabiscuit.

Soon, everyone began wondering if
that had been a big mistake.

Seabiscuit was fat—200 pounds
overweight! He was nervous and
snapped at the jockeys. He got crazy if
anybody tried to put a saddle on him.

And he slept too much! Most horses sleep standing up. Sometimes they lie down, but only for a few minutes at a time. Not Seabiscuit. He would flop over in his stall and snooze for hours. In the morning, the trainers couldn't wake him up.

Even worse, Seabiscuit seemed to hate his new home. He paced back and forth in his stall. He would not eat. He kicked and bit. Nobody wanted to go near him!

Tom Smith, however, thought he knew of a way to make Seabiscuit feel at home.

First, he knocked down one wall
of his stall to make more room. Then
he brought in a friendly old cow pony,
a small stray dog, and a spider monkey
named Jo Jo.

Something amazing happened. This
odd group of animals became friends
with Seabiscuit. They even slept together
in the stall. Seabiscuit calmed down.

Smith did something else. He showered Seabiscuit with affection. He spent hours training him. He even slept in the barn at times.

Slowly, he began to understand this
spirited, misunderstood horse. And
Seabiscuit began to show Tom Smith what
he could do.

At last, Seabiscuit was ready for his first
big race. It was in Detroit, Michigan. A
big crowd turned out to watch. Nobody
thought Seabiscuit could win—nobody
except Tom Smith.

And everybody was amazed when Seabiscuit did win—everybody except Tom Smith.

Seabiscuit showed the world what he could do. When he really wanted to race, he ran like lightning.

That day was only the beginning.

Seabiscuit's home for the winter was in
California. He rode to the West Coast in a
private train car. He had it all to himself.
There was plenty to eat, plenty of room
to walk around, and plenty of hay to
sleep in!

The big race in California was called
the Santa Anita Handicap. First prize was
$100,000!

On the day of the race, fourteen horses lined up at the starting line. Thousands of people were in the stands. Most thought a horse named Rosemont would win.

The bell rang, the crowd cheered, and the horses shot out of the gates!

Halfway around the mile-long track, Seabiscuit made his move. He went from fourth place to third place. From third place to second place. By the time the horses reached the homestretch, Seabiscuit was out in front!

Then something happened.

For some reason, Seabiscuit did not notice that Rosemont was coming up behind him. Suddenly, the race was a tie between Seabiscuit and Rosemont. They crossed the finish line together.

"Seabiscuit won!" shouted some people. "Rosemont won!" others cried.

Who was right?

A photo taken at the finish line showed what really happened. The winner was Rosemont. The big race had turned out to be a big loss for Seabiscuit.

But Seabiscuit got over it. That summer, he won race after race.

Huge crowds began to show up at the track.

They were not interested in the other horses anymore. Everyone was rooting for Seabiscuit!

The year was 1936. The country was having a hard time. It was the Great Depression. Many people could not find jobs. Seabiscuit gave them hope.

If that little horse can do it, they thought, *then so can I.*

When Seabiscuit took the train back to California, it seemed as if everybody in the country knew his name. At every stop along the way, people lined up to see him.

Stories about Seabiscuit ran in news-
papers and magazines. His picture was
everywhere. Seabiscuit was not just
a racehorse anymore. He was a celebrity.

People played Seabiscuit board games.
They put their money in Seabiscuit
wallets. They wore Seabiscuit hats.

Soon it was time for Seabiscuit to race in the Santa Anita Handicap in California again. This time, when Seabiscuit walked to the starting line, the crowd was cheering for him over all the other horses!

"They're off!" yelled the man behind the microphone.

Twelve horses left the gates. Next to Seabiscuit, another horse tripped. He slammed into Seabiscuit. Now the only way Seabiscuit could catch up was to run as hard as he could, right from the start.

But that was risky. A horse that runs hard at the starting line can be too tired to win at the finish. Seabiscuit, however, caught up anyway.

Now Seabiscuit and one other horse stayed in front all the way down the homestretch. They crossed the finish line together.

Once again, Seabiscuit lost by a nose!

For the second time in a row, the "big race" was bad luck for Seabiscuit. Even so, he was still a star.

The only horse that was more famous than the horse named Seabiscuit was a horse named War Admiral. War Admiral looked like a real racehorse. He ran like one, too. War Admiral almost never lost a race. People started to wonder: *What would happen if Seabiscuit and War Admiral were in a race together?*

War Admiral

So a "match race" was arranged. That means only two horses are on the track.

All over the country, millions of people stopped what they were doing to listen to the race on the radio. Even President Franklin D. Roosevelt! He was supposed to hold a press conference—but he made all the reporters wait until the race was over.

The two horses walked out on the track together. Seabiscuit and War Admiral. Their riders talked on the way. Then they reached the starting line . . . and took off like a couple of rockets!

Most people thought War Admiral
would start faster than Seabiscuit.
But it was the other way around.

Seabiscuit got off to a faster start.
And stayed there!

Then they got to the homestretch. War Admiral came around the outside. They were neck and neck.

Seabiscuit's rider looked over and saw something in War Admiral's face. The horse was running out of steam.

"So long, Charley!" yelled Seabiscuit's rider to the other jockey.

Seabiscuit crossed the finish line—
alone.

The crowd went wild!

It was a great day for Seabiscuit.

But soon after this wonderful victory, everything started to go wrong.

Seabiscuit was getting ready for his third try to win the Santa Anita Handicap. In a "practice" race, Seabiscuit's rider heard something snap. Seabiscuit kept going. He seemed okay . . . until he got to the finish line.

As soon as Seabiscuit stopped, he held
his weight off one leg.

Tom Smith ran onto the track.
Seabiscuit was hurt!

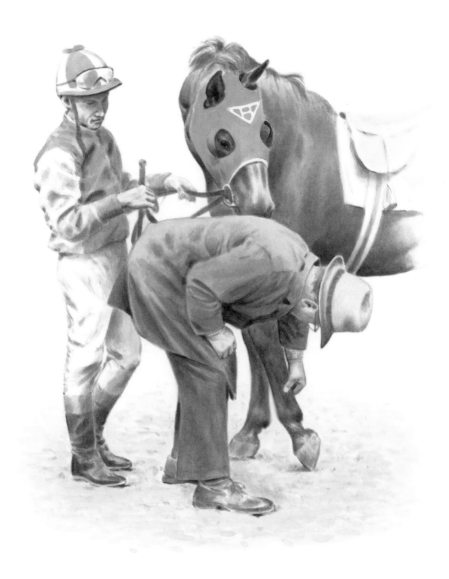

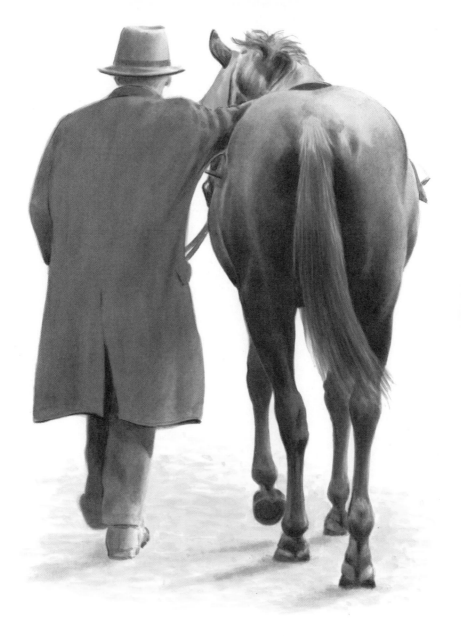

Everyone who loved Seabiscuit was
heartbroken. His racing days were surely
over. Seabiscuit went home to rest. But
he didn't like resting.

Slowly, his leg began to heal. He started
chasing deer all around the ranch.

Seabiscuit wanted to race again. Could
he do it?

No horse with this kind of injury had ever come back. But Seabiscuit was a special racehorse.

In 1940, Seabiscuit came out to run one more race. One more time he would try to win the Santa Anita Handicap. He was twice as old as most of the other horses. He hadn't run a race in a year.

But when the horses came around the backstretch, Seabiscuit was right behind the two leaders.

Suddenly, he squeezed through the middle. Then he blasted off and won!

He had won the Santa Anita Handicap at last.

In six years, Seabiscuit had won 33
races. He had won more prize money
than any other racehorse in history.

After that, Seabiscuit "retired." He was
brought home to the ranch. He took it
easy. He had fun chasing cattle around.

And he greeted the nearly 50,000 fans who came to visit him.

On May 17, 1947, Seabiscuit died at the age of 14. He was buried at the ranch. And that is where he rests—that wonderful, funny-looking horse called Seabiscuit.